D1487487

AMBUSHES AND APOLOGIES

AMBUSHES AND APOLOGIES

by

James Magorian

THE IBIS PRESS
Chicago

"Have some wine?" the March Hare said in an encouraging tone.

Alice looked all round the table, but there was nothing on it but tea. "I don't see any wine," she remarked.

"There isn't any," said the March Hare.

— Lewis Carroll

[*v*]

CONTENTS

AMBUSHES AND APOLOGIES

MARCH

march is fading
from the corner
of an empty field
  the far room
  of a schoolyard
sun-bent snow
leaves an afternoon
of mud
  and pools
  of water
holding
  a thin surface
  of ice
patches of pale grass
swish in the wind
   homework assignments
   and paper cups
tumbleweed
  across the soft ground
spring
  brings noise
  and footprints

THE GENERAL

sargon of akkad
solemnly parked
his scythed chariot
in his reserved stall
and dreamed his way
across the parade ground
where hate
was being issued
to new recruits
he smiled past
the numbered barracks
dismal and obedient
and entered
the pilastered temple
where all altars
must be mirrors
walking giantly
in his glittering
ribbon-soaked uniform
through long halls
worshipped with pictures
of old weapons
and fallen heroes
he stepped boldly
briefcase heavy
with patriotic slogans
into his opulent
leather-licensed office
placed his sword
on top of a file cabinet
and sat down
at his ambitious desk
crowned with telephones
and toy cannons
lit a cigar
looked at his calendar
and ordered
the war to begin

ODYSSEUS IN A CRUMPLED SUIT

an old man
　　　from
the pigeon benches
　　　walking
　　　　　　slowly
with a twisted cane
　　　walking
　　　　　　slowly
down dearborn street
　　　walking
　　　　　　slowly
across the bridge
　　　into
the once
　　　of a city

FIRST AND LAST

the sun
sends
shadows

through
the orchard

another day
clicks
into place

flying reptiles
from jurassic
skies

splash
in pools
of morning
rain

the front
gate
opens

maecenas
walks slowly
up the path
with sacks
of gold
to buy
a poem

HECATE'S MOUNTAIN

timber-howl endurance
between new moons
    wishing
on the rim of promise
    spinning
the loyalty of chance
into the silver stupor
of an opium mind
    remembering
the fluted surface
of faded grief
    forgetting
the hedge-hiding ambushes
of harmonic gunfire
    lion mountain
    an answer of cliffs
    an answer of trees

TELL ME AGAIN

gadget-man
tell me again
how great you are
i saw the child
hit by the car
tell me again
how you fixed the door
you forgot to mention the war
tell me again
you are innately good
i visited hiroshima
as everyone should
tell me again
your way is lighted
by golden lamps
i have retraced your steps
to the torture camps
tell me again
you are one
of the chosen people
i saw the city smoke
on the steeple
tell me again
of your divine fate
i heard the words
of street-corner hate
tell me again   no
do not tell me again

GHETTO SONG

a delicate row
of glass bottles
glitters warmly
on a cracked sidewalk

across the street
a vacant lot
grows a garden
of broken bricks

dark buildings echo
with the sounds
of breaking glass
and children's shouts

innocent laughter
and running feet
move down the street
toward other castles

ARGUMENT

with summer
snarling
in angry suns
at the velocity
of sacrifices
without ends
the question
of progress
swept through
our expanding
conversation
and when
words ended
zeno had
to remove
an arrow
from my back

GOODBYE

the days
untouched
by plans
are gone

yesterdays
are revised
to describe
new wounds

tomorrows
rest only
upon proper
membership

calibrated
eyes record
the wrong
resurrection

analyses
of love are
published
quarterly

no images
survive
the science
of roses

scholarly
teeth ruin
the ocean's
reputation

some things
left unsaid
gather near
fresh graves

SUGGESTION

the hidden
and prating
procedures
of the unconscious
design content
and technique
and leave behind
many meanings
for the epidemic
of criticism
and if art
and neurosis
depart from
the world
by the same
dark exit
in unknown allegiance
to the kingdom
of childhood
then imagination
is broken memory
and metaphors
are false
messengers

SAND DUNES

twisted shelf
of sandpipers
and sea gulls

low tide falls
to salt shores
of beach plums

beached seaweed
anchors a ridge
in leeward hope

numbered origins
summon innocence
to its execution

caged sea replies
with white whirls
of moon skeletons

PROMISE

summer messages written on the wind
and delivered anxiously to searching senses
    time and wind
      dignity and pretensions
      leaking assumptions
      escaping events

condemning jury of pine trees
shedding long needles of sorrow
      iron leaves
      exhausted clocks
      new roads
      sad endings

fluttering brown farewells of sparrows slowly
scattering across the road and into the cornfield
      school days
      autumn
      river fugitives
      campfires

recently cut field of wheat
with rain-drop noise on all sides
      heat and fragrance
      time and light
      home
      forgiveness

three pieces of whispering geography
that eternity loaned to summer
        mountain graves
        river buoy
        prairie cairn
        rendezvous

THE EMPIRE OF THOUGHT

on all levels
an idea
without pardon

designed by
the best
and worst

captured by
warmth
and motion

bends too far
toward
simplicity

and falls
soundlessly
into

the cradle
of cruelty

I CAN'T HEAR YOU

a
fang-spread
cycle
of syllables
cleaves
blood-sheltered
angles
of escape
because
promises
are
mirrors reversed
and
innocent images
always
dance
in the light
of lies

SALE

the sun
sold
for whispered
reasons
disappears
into
the whirling
retreat
of apology

AFTERNOON

the pigeons
crowd
the edge
of the roof
to watch
the children
of distance
and music
construct
a fence
of autumn
leaves
to house
their giraffe
while across
the street
an old man
moves his chair
from the shade
into the sunlight

DIAGRAM OF TIME

inside seasons
      bent north
      with care
the flesh-delivered
              designs
of a debt of rage
          collect
a certain universe
where abbreviations
cancel spoken colors
and paste gold stars
on a progress chart

DEATH IN THE FOREST

faded blue
faded brown
searching for eagles
in the high cliffs
following the tracks
of a wolf
along water-carved ravines
careless
among the sinister sounds
of time
famous in their mixture
and indulgent of distance
saber-winged hawks
cast
sweeping shadows
on the forest floor
crows calling
over the next hill
icy creek jerking
through the canyon
intense
in winding zeal
chipmunks
run along the bluffs
gray trees
spread legends
of green
shields of bark
peeling from dead trees
peeling from dreams and madness
useless followers
give faint suggestions
for paper substitutes
volcanic crown of thorns
authentic until subversive wishes
appear in symphonies

snow-spotted hillside
        burned by omnipotence
        in drifting pattern
damp logs
rotting stumps
turning into powder
to be stolen
by the wind
        a handful
        of leaves
        wet and cold
                the brown mosaic
                of last autumn's deaths
great grasping branches
                of ambition
reaching out but never arriving
        no gods
        no sins
time lost
stump-shredded
in the funeral forest
                confessional
        and mysterious
long mesopotamian journal
of broken trees
        predominance
of pyramid radiance
        occasional reasons
        toward forgiveness
the vigilance of vindication
lines of exchange
                by ear
                not by formula
a walking disguise
a shelter of escape
from betrayed seasons
from betrayed self

IN THE BEGINNING

north of sheridan
outside the reach
of high mountains
lost and cautious
in spring shadows
behind the broken
surfaces of night
a bitter farewell
erodes the levels
of runaway dreams
with wild glances
glazed by despair
and shy upheavals
of cruel whispers

THE CIRCLES OF IOWA

in the early morning
when winter walks
through the easy hills
among the many shades
of brown and yellow
that linger beneath
the gray november sky
osage orange trees
stand above circles
of abandoned children
and old wagon wheels
painted white lean against
trees and fence posts
while red-faced farmers
haul wagons of grain
along narrow roads
that wind endlessly

FUNERAL

the capricious solitudes
of ritualistic sympathy
sacrificially cancel
the cruel adjectives
written on the mind
but never spoken
and this conspiracy
of unread audiences
displays the best power
proving conclusively
that unctuous sobriety
and famous restraint
do not ultimately decide
who weeps for whom
in ordered superstition

LAKE FLAMBEAU

along the ledge
above the lake
green to blue
over bleaching bones
that once were trees
along the ledge
above the lake
day to night
with a driftwood visor
to search the valley
of the fast falling sun
along the ledge
above the lake
summer to fall
wishing the distant trees
could support the sun
a moment longer
along the ledge
above the lake
present to past
late investments
deposited in eternity

WAITING

cold wind
of delicate doom
black rainbow
of secrets
told in whispers
by candlelight
praising red
praising darkness
three persuasions
of summer vision
sold for hope
outside dimensions
outside the rules
of circumstance

JUPITER

the selfish days
of grandeur
and decay
caught under
the brief lens
of poetry
sparkle
with evil
as tautologies
fall into
lonely focus
and the casual
warnings
of forms
with almost shapes
and eastern homes
go unheeded
in the eclectic
land of sun
and sea

APRIL SNOWFALL

south birds
betrayed
in a late
cold regret
sad while
white wind
covers hope
leaving
a shelf
of snow
on the long
stone steps
winding
to the lake

NEAR GRANDVIEW

tall buildings
are hiding
in the fog
    business towers
    smokestacks
    cathedral spires
hanging
        gray
across the river
in the absence
of the sun

       cities
exist only
in the distance
    no one
ever gets close
    to them
a street
a house
a few faces
    followed
    by the selection
    of ruins
    and the blades
    of history

NEBRASKA

a hundred lonely
 dreams
  beyond
the city limits
of fort kearney
  ghost herds
   of buffalo
  graze
   on summer slopes
morning wind
  sweeps
across muddy fields
  jaggedly lined
by the tearing
steel touch
  of shining plows
meadowlarks sail
   over prairie sod
a soft song
  shatters the sky

WAITING ROOM

for the cambered people
sitting in silence
counting the categories
of identification
and casually thinking
of the short interval
from initial survival
to complete domination
the question concerning
the relative proportions
of spirit and matter
resulted in the final
intellectual convulsions
and the cyclical arrival
of the uniformed shaman

RAIN FOREST

damp soft world
cut by glaciers
in four visions
of eyeless pain

fir and hemlock
censor sunlight
for sword ferns
and wood sorrel

arches of vines
form cathedrals
of sitka spruce
and blood cedar

raindrops cling
with cold grasp
to incantations
of silent claws

the dense shade
of tangled time
records its own
level of motive

LOST LANGUAGE

in slow progression
the simple cries
of savage animals
were followed
by the omniscient
floating songs
of the senses
and this joyous
cosmic connection
of sounds
and desires
was then captured
by the ominous
list of endeavors
and communication
was destroyed

FIELD

the long shadows
of afternoon
sway through
green-hedged hills
walked by old women
in bright scarfs
slowly making
stacks of grain
with wooden rakes
for stoic horses
to haul away
in weathered wagons
to village markets

GRAVESIDE

when curiosity died
to the tune
of a twelve-tone wind
near a cold and faded
stone age painting
the clever tongues
of ambiguity
arrived to deliver
the funeral oration
carrying a basket
of conspiracy

the pageant was colorful
but of little interest
until i discovered
that i was the one
they were burying

VISITING HOURS

on sunday
afternoon
the halls
are filled
with eyes
and noise
as people
parade past
the glass
questions
ignoring
the message
related by
the row
of skulls
in the basement
exhibition
leaving
fingerprints
paper cups
half-smoked
cigarettes
and echoes
to record
their boredom

ARK

look forward
look backward
in an effort
to see again
the mystical
commandments
that crossed
an achievement
of repetition
and found life
at that hard
prairie school
complexity
one and many
the same faces
of the crowd
with revelation
into midnight
dampness
with dark trees
walking along
the street
of vines
from knowledge
into knowledge

SEQUENCE

the children
of anarchy
carry coins
of history
to purchase
recognition
when cities
disappear
and rituals
are changed

ESTABLISHED TESTIMONY

standing
in the doorway
the smiling child
with brown
and tangled hair
watched the wind
twist yellow leaves
across the autumn
afternoon
and down
the vanishing paths
of october days
piling them against
black iron fences
and covering
the brick sidewalks
sculptured by
time and travel
with a layer
of autumn tears

INFORMATION

the gargoyle knowledge
is guilefully placed
on punched cards
and plastic tapes

our problems climb
into steel boxes
and gambol through
electronic relays

the clicking answers
hide a cynical laugh
and mention savages
huddled near a fire
making poison arrows

at six o'clock
the janitor sweeps out
the ignorance

MORNING

everything is hiding
in the mist
white houses stand
without doors
without windows
the wet grass
shivers
in the windy dark
and prays
for the sun
the river has
only one bank
where cottonwoods
watch
the wall of gray
from water
to sky
from water
to eternity
dampness
haze
morning

OFFICIAL SHELTER

the traveler
laughed loudly
and knocked down
the road sign
as the zealous
silhouettes leaned
toward the west
grasping marvelous
green manuscripts
and promising new
identities while
in the background
a procession filed
to that familiar
canyon rim where
bearded poets
play prophet
in the sunset

BOATS

when april appears
along the river
to apologize
for the rage
of winter
small boats
are lifted
off racks
and pulled
to the water's edge
in preparation
for the slow
poisonous voyages
of summer ritual

RETURN

the disheveled bark
of the cedar tree
and the despair
of the dust-covered lilacs
ally with invisible elms
lost cornfields
and empty vineyards
to mark ancient paths
that lead around
the corners of memory
to old hiding places
torn open for passageways
to long tables
standing in museum silence
stealing space from
the innocent rooms
surrounding floors
of thin worn boards
to encroaching partitions
in the flower's shadow
covered with religious pictures
to the wall
where a map of palestine
replaced the durand painting
and to the abandoned hours
of the sun
that are never found
by searching parties

DANDELIONS

behind the cautious bridge
below the hideous symbols
my nefarious neighbor
made prefatory remarks
about the weather
and then with a myriad
of sacerdotal gestures
suggested the most efficient
procedure for removing
the flock of dandelions
from my generous garden

slowly lowering my eyes
to the summer ground
and feeling the distance
between us grow and echo
i thought of those vague
strategies of the mind
that mix harsh heredity
with varied experience
to construct separate
visions of the same object
to cause my neighbor
to see only invading evil
where i saw only splendor

GHOST TOWN

cold mornings of rain
in haystack memories
of mountain shadows

long nightmare journal
of local extinctions
written with blood
in gliding grammar
by ancient scribes
faithfully recording
the killing season
and its exiled cast
of bitter characters

red hills revenge
distances of escape
in vultures' stare

THE LONG RESULT

a new
    curriculum
but
the same
    delirium

a prayer
    for
        lenience
while ideals
float under
        convenience

the search
    of
empty motion
    for
lost devotion

the long
    result
  of
silent assault
is youth forged
and lions gorged

TIPPECANOE

a lonely summer sun
lingers in sympathy
along narrow water
where continents ago
in desperate defense
of life and land
the chipped flints
of savagery erected
bitter boundaries
of blackened blood

FRAGMENT AND VARIATION

colored consequences
splash briefly across
everlasting inquiries
and brightly designate
the unknown strategies
and the long vague
pusillanimous tactics
that toss red spears
from the cold roadside
and recommend a quick
and unnoticed death
instead of the slow execution
of a dry and fading curl
on a green desk top
under the electric eyes
of almost remediable souls

FOR THOMAS JEFFERSON

arrogant practice
betrays ideals
and classical
necessities
explain shy
paradoxes
if the waves
of belief
distribute
extinctions
as equal
is equal
and equal
is nothing
to assertions
of doom
over doom
and justice
and mercy
for mozart
in the sad
circumference
of fire
and the
splinters
of dreams
only

WABASH WAGON

in dark abandonment
at the contrite end
of a sinuous
and greenly crowded
soybean field
a broken wagon
leans indolently
against an empty
barn of weathered
and warped boards
and sadly displays
the rustic scars
of violent extortion
while four trees
east of its shadow
secure in a shore
of muddy promises
a pond whispers
to weeping willows
and goldenrods
as the wind erases
duck trails from
its silver surface

ONTOLOGY

the wind caught
the wild sounds
of civilization
and threw
their structure
against the wall
unquestioned
structures shift
structures fade
structures depart
but underneath
immutable forms
where there
is no time
and eternity
is secularized
adversaries
celebrate
the end
of history
and the unity
of repetition
and novelty

PETERSBURG BATTLEFIELD

gardens wild with color
unlock a distant meadow
of heat and silence
where angry armies
plundered the wind
with violent pieces
of cancelled sound
and left their blood
for a small museum
of summer visitors

AEDILES

inundating darkness
ancient fears
gathering years
liquid suns
flowing skies
creative codes
personal marks
plates of gold
angry tribes
in loose completion
false analogies
protect precision
cradle and crucifix
a faint confession
bending definitions
in orgiastic protest
with shadowy severity
with wordless curves
the angry relics
of neglected tradition
breathe regret
and cavernously cast
a funeral smile
for the particles
of radiant energy
angel wings selling
intergalactic space
pendulous thoughts
beyond a system
among ghostly years
of private tears
where the justification
of all visions
is the preservation
of surviving wonder

GUESTS

desperate
in a vast
intention
the guests
measured
the doubt
in spikes
of barley
in swift
assassins
in bloody
entrails
of an owl
in books
of wind
and idle
thunder
in clicks
of machines
and then told
the wolf
where
the lamb
was hiding

MOUNTAIN

with
all images
frozen
now
by art
the gray
snow-winged
mountain
becomes
a ceremony

JOSHUA TREES

waned and lost
in oxen dust
wandering tribes
tent-strained
and revealed
discover joshua trees
in sand-tender temples
worshipped
and mourning
miracled into saints
miscible flight
of spirit
and flesh
with marvelous
upstretched branches
white-clustered
praying green
and drifted
in a great guarded
seething desert
of shaggy sheep
and lengths of lizards
where fire
and wind
lend altars
to judging pilgrims

STABERN STREET

a boy
stands
beside
his bicycle

on a worn
and winding
cobblestone
street

looking
into
the cold
gray
stillness
of a winter
morning

his eyes
glazed
with wonder

his dreams
dancing
in the mist

SONG OF SUMMER

locked
inside
the song
of summer
warm winds
raid
rain-tangled
trees
decorated
with
black rebellions
of rough-throated
crows

RAIN

a wind-wounded
concerto of rain
seizes the silence
of twilight
and drowns time
in a puddle
of muddy water
at the edge
of a sidewalk

SILVER COINS AND A SPUR

6 o'clock breakfast
in quiet darkness

mending fences
in mountain wind

quit work early
for saturday night

lights of town
glow contemptuously

another whiskey
to celebrate

the hanging
of a rustler

and the blizzard
of '87

drunken cowboy
lassoing legends

on a broken street
in butte montana

obedient horse
tied to a hitching rail

silver coins and a spur
lost in the mud

long cold ride
back to the ranch

THE WRONG KINGDOM

recurrent cries
carefully scheduled
in the night

achieve conversion
by systems
passed from grace

gentle waves
alter cobwebbed
tunnels

for others
to touch
with values

but never
enter

EXPANSION

sleepless reward
hanging from trees
       music
   in the wind
words surrounding words
   night
        of
           stone
beyond the letter
    of all events
so fragrant
so deserted
    the construction
    of ruins
for myth
from smoke
in the pulse of rain
    by swan-benches
bending the terror
    of the tongue
standing tall in time
climbing the broken rungs
    of private ladders
   toward other voices
we should have left earlier